NOT SO LONG AGO

Rhoades photographed Utica's landmark First Church of Christ, Scientist draped with an impressive American flag during World War II. This building became the new home of the Oneida County Historical Society in 1991.

6/20/44 21155

NOT SO LONG AGO

UTICA AND VICINITY, 1940—1949

Photographs from the Russell Rhoades Collection

Compiled by Eleanor "Peg" Hassett

Foreword by Douglas M. Preston

ONEIDA COUNTY HISTORICAL SOCIETY
UTICA, NEW YORK

North Country Books, Inc.
Utica, New York

NOT SO LONG AGO

UTICA AND VICINITY, 1940 – 1949

Photographs from the
Russell Rhoades Collection

ISBN 978-1-4930-7681-9

Library of Congress Cataloging-in-Publication Data

Hassett, Eleanor, 1917-
Not so long ago : Utica and vicinity 1940-1949 / compiled by
Eleanor "Peg" Hassett.
p. c.m.
ISBN 978-1-4930-7681-9 (pbk.)
1. Utica (N.Y.)—Social life and customs—Pictorial works.
2. Utica Region (N.Y.)—Social life and customs—Pictorial works.
I. Title.
F129.U8H36 1992
974.7'62—dc20 92-35781
CIP

Published by
North Country Books, Inc.
18 Irving Place
Utica, New York 13501-5618

In Memory of
Mary Louise Quayle

Peg Hassett, left, and Mary Louise Quayle examine negatives in the Rhoades collection.
6/5/87 Courtesy *Observer-Dispatch*

Russell and Helen Rhoades, with son Tommy.

Table of Contents

Foreword

One of the great pleasures of working in a historical society is being present at the discovery of lost treasures, especially when the discovery is unexpected. Our discovery of the Russell Rhoades collection began in 1981 when Patrick Peterson approached the Oneida County Historical Society for help in researching the history of the Savage Arms Corporation in Utica, specifically the experiences of Savage workers during the busy days of World War II. The Society obtained a mini-grant in support of this project from the New York Historical Resources Center at Cornell University.

In the course of Pat's research he discovered that Savage had published a newsletter—*The Totem Pole*—illustrated with photos by Russell Rhoades, showing people at work, company baseball and bowling teams, War Bond drives, etc. Hoping to develop a slide program or an exhibition on Savage Arms, we contacted the Russell Rhoades Company on the off chance that they might still have the original Savage negatives.

Not only did they still have them, but thousands more. Even a cursory examination of the contents of dozens of rusty filing cabinets disclosed one treasure after another: downtown Utica before Urban Renewal and the arterials, long-vanished factories churning out the arms of war and the goods of peace, auto showrooms filled with Detroit's finest, even a shot of the landmark Kewpee's hamburger stand on Oneida Square.

It has been more than a decade since the Rhoades collection first came to our attention. Time was needed, first to take physical possession and secure ownership of the collection through the courtesy of Joseph Skane, the current president of the Russell Rhoades Company. Then, beginning in 1985, Peg Hassett, the late Mary Louise Quayle, and George White sorted, refiled and cataloged the collection. They were aided by a 1986 grant for supplies, materials and equipment from the Helen Ney Best Crouse Fund of the Utica Foundation, Inc. Without the work of these dedicated volunteers and the support of the Utica Foundation, this book would not have been possible. Mrs. Hassett and Mr. White have also put the experience gained with this collection to work on other OCHS negative collections, some acquired since the Rhoades collection, and some long before.

From the day we first saw this treasure trove in Rhoades' basement, we hoped to do a book based on it. Selected images were used in the now-out-of-print volume, *The Upper Mohawk Country: An Illustrated History of Greater Utica*, published in 1982, and in a number of other OCHS exhibits and programs.

But the book idea remained on the back burner while the Society searched for, secured, remodelled and relocated to its new home in the former Christian Science Church. With "the move" behind us, we can turn our attention to such projects as this, and are pleased to offer *Not So Long Ago* as our first major publication from our new location. Any profits from the sale of this book will help to further develop the Society's efforts "to collect and commemorate the history of Central New York in general and the County of Oneida in particular."

—*Douglas M. Preston*
Director

Introduction

About 1934, Utica native Russell T. Rhoades established a business for commercial, industrial and insurance photography; his company carried on this general type of work until 1958, when they bought out the John Barnard Blueprint Co. at 27 Devereux Street and began to specialize in architectural services. Most of the photos were not taken for artistic reasons, but they were made on large format cameras with considerable skill. Outdoor scenes in particular show a vanished Utica that is still within the memory of many people.

Fortunately, these photos were made on safety film rather than with the notoriously flammable nitrate film. However, this early safety film has its own drawbacks; the cellulose di- or tri-acetate film base sometimes shrinks, causing the gelatin emulsion layer to reticulate or form thick ridges. With this collection, the process was hastened by fires in both adjoining buildings on Devereux Street and subsequent flooding of Rhoades' basement. At that time, many negatives were irretrievably lost. Others show more or less damage but are still important sources of historical information.

Enough excellent negatives survived the dangers of fire, flood and poor storage conditions to allow us to limit the contents of this book to the years 1940-1949. There are even more photos available from the period 1950-1960 and we hope to publish a selection of them in a future volume. Each photo or group of photos is identified with a brief caption, a date, and Rhoades' original file number.

Some of the dates shown with the photos are obviously "out of synch" with the weather conditions depicted. We believe that in many cases these are the dates when the negatives were filed, rather than when they were taken. The reader can assume that a picture was taken no later than the date shown, but may have been taken anywhere from a few days to a few months earlier.

Also, we have not included identifications of all individuals. Although we have full or partial (usually last name only) information on some of the people in these pictures, we did not feel that most were of sufficient general interest to include, especially when we lack such information for the great majority of the images. However, we would appreciate receiving more such information for our records.

For some of you, we hope this volume will provide many good memories; for others, an introduction to the Utica area of your parents' or grandparents' day. Enjoy!

—*Peg Hassett*

Late afternoon shadows were long at the Busy Corner.
10/9/40 19576

Downtown

Downtown was where the action was; this was where we went for serious shopping or to meet friends for lunch, where doctors and lawyers and insurance people had their offices, where we could enjoy a night out, where the boys went to watch the girls and where the girls went to be watched. The Busy Corner earned its name.

Here we have defined downtown as the area from Bagg's Square and Union Station to South Street, and from State Street to John Street.

This aerial view of Utica shows a busy, crowded area with no parking lots. We know it was taken a few years before the filing date (1947) because at least one of the structures had been demolished by then.

The key will help to identify the buildings:

1. *Savings Bank of Utica*
2. *City Hall*
3. *Grace Episcopal Church*
4. *First Bank and Trust Company*
5. *First National Bank Building*
6. *Hotel Utica*
7. *Devereux Block*
8. *Insurance Building*
9. *Hotel Hamilton (Hotel Martin)*
10. *St. John's Church*
11. *Utica Catholic Academy*
12. *Central Fire Station*
13. *Boys' Trade School*
14. *Oneida County Courthouse*
15. *Assumption Academy*
16. *Oneida Historical Society*

8/19/47 23143

On Lafayette Street were hotels, restaurants and movie houses as well as shops. The junction with Genesee Street was the west side of the Busy Corner.
6/1/44 21130B

The east side of the Busy Corner was the intersection of Bleecker Street with Genesee. Looming behind Daw's Drug Store was the Oneida National Bank; St. John's Church and Ribyat's Furniture store were in the distance.
6/1/44 21130A

The Arcade Building, long a fixture of downtown Utica, was being demolished.
1/18/41 18827

The facade of the Boston Store stood in place of the Arcade Building.
7/22/41 19322

Sidewalk superintendents watched the construction of the Boston Store closely. Burlesque reigned at the Colonial Theater.
6/2/42 19186

60 YEARS
OF
WOOLWORTH
IN UTICA
FEB. 22ND 1879
F.W. WOOLWORTH
Opened his FIRST
5¢ store in the Old ARCADE Building
here in UTICA – His Opening Stock
$315 WORTH OF MERCHANDISE
IN THIS WINDOW ARE SOME OF THE

8/3/40 18138

Genesee Street was the principal route for through as well as local traffic. This block just south of the Busy Corner was always crowded with cars and people.
9/20/40 18425

The First National Bank Building was Utica's skyscraper. Kresge's was on the ground floor.
10/30/40 18552

This handsome building stood at 100 Genesee Street.
11/26/40 18694

This row of stores was at 54-60 Genesee Street.
1/4/43 20274

The barber pole at 29 Genesee Street announced the location of John F. White's establishment.
6/7/41 19243

Philipson's Army and Navy was then at 88-90 Genesee Street.
10/14/40 18476

Oriskany Street West was the site of smaller shops and the popular Imperial Restaurant. It was a major east-west throroughfare.
5/22/44 21091

The New York Bakery was on Whitesboro Street when this photo was taken.
5/24/44 21115

This business on the northeast corner of Bleecker and John Streets was well known to many residents.
6/22/43 20529B

Hotel Martin on Oriskany Street had been sold and was soon to be called Hotel Hamilton. There was also a Bleecker Street entrance.
1/27/43 20882B

The diner on Oriskany Street near the hotel was showing its age.
5/22/44 21091E

The mezzanine of the Hotel Martin was a quiet place when this picture was taken.
5/17/44 21066E

The Grill Room of the hotel was a popular eating and socializing spot.
1/27/44 20882C

This parking meter on Bleecker Street provided a handy hitch for a horse.
1/27/44 20882A

Downtown had many grocery stores. This one was at 331 Columbia Street.
5/15/42 20015

Then as now, snow removal was sometimes a problem. This view was from State Street looking east on Lafayette Street.
2/24/41 18989

No snow this December, and Maher Brothers had the only holiday decorations in this view of Seneca Street, looking north toward the Hotel Utica.
12/22/40 18779B

The Hotel Pershing adjoined the Hotel Utica on Lafayette Street.
6/9/42 20088

Smoking chimneys northeast of the Busy Corner indicated plenty of manufacturing activity. In the foreground were the Colonial Theater and the Hotel Hamilton.
5/1/44 21066A

Utica percale sheets were featured at a local store.
4/29/43 20455B

The sales ladies of the J.B. Wells cosmetics section posed nicely.
3/28/47 22820 (damaged)

Berger's at Columbia and Cornelia Streets was noted for bargain tables.
5/15/42 20016

Helen Hoffman conducted business at her newsstand on the Columbia Street side of the First Bank and Trust building for many years, rain or shine.
3/23/41 19044

A shopkeeper watched the passing scene on Genesee Street, south of Bank Place.
6/25/40 17978

Dunham Station of the Post Office was in this building at 254 Genesee Street, next door below the Fort Schuyler Club. It later lost its handsome terra cotta cornice.
4/23/43 20452B

Many people remember Miss Ruth Auert at her desk in the Savings Bank.
1/22/43 20319

These stores, 192-204 Genesee Street, came down for urban renewal in the early 1970s to become the site of the Sheraton, later Radisson, Hotel.
9/1/43 20592A

On the east side of Genesee Street, the State Office Building replaced these buildings.
7/11/43 20548

Central New York Power Company occupied the lower floor of this imposing building at Genesee and Court Streets. On the upper floors were many doctors' and dentists' offices. Farther down Court Street, Central Methodist Church had no steeple at that time.
5/8/44 21114

The cashier's window for Central New York Power Company was discreetly placed in this large lobby where the latest appliances were on display.
5/8/44 21114

The Fisher Building at 262 Genesee Street was replaced by the Cornhill Savings and Loan Association, later County Federal, and still later, Dime Savings.
5/7/49 22890

At 267 Genesee Street, just south of the Stanley Theater, C.J. Fletcher was ready to sell Nash cars.
5/22/47 22911C

John T. Buckley Pool at Albany Street, Culver Avenue and Welshbush Road was added to T.R. Proctor Park by the WPA and became a haven for East Utica youngsters in summer.
6/20/44 21149A

The Neighborhoods

We lived in the neighborhoods, bought necessities and some luxuries from the corner store, attended school within a few blocks of home and went to the small theaters for second run films. Each area had its own focus and its own ethnic flavor; some were primarily commercial but most were residential. All were tied to downtown and to each other first by streetcars and then by buses. Many people still lived in the neighborhoods where they grew up.

The Soldiers and Sailors Monument was still the hub of Oneida Square.
1940 17974

Many Uticans remember the appetizing fragrance and taste of a Kewpee hamburger.
6/47 23089

Faculty members of the newly established Utica College stand in the arch of Plymouth Congregational Church, where some classes were held.
2/27/47 22701

Adjoining residences of the F. T. and T. R. Proctor families housed the Munson-Williams-Proctor Institute for many years.
6/20/46 21156B

Art at the Institute contrasted sharply with the Victorian home.
11/14/41 19672

This streetcar was travelling north on Genesee Street under the green arcade of elms, approaching Noyes Street on the right.
6/28/40 17894

Looking north, this was the view of Genesee Street from the Kanatenah apartments. The stately elm trees had to be cut down when Dutch elm disease invaded the area.
10/9/40 18432

Like most neighborhood theaters, the Uptown in South Utica used prizes and games to attract viewers.
9/8/41 19394

2/24/41 18982

The Lyons estate at 2710 Genesee Street became the site of Temple Emanu-El.
5/20/43 20491

The streetcar tracks on Mohawk Street had been removed, but were still evident. Here the view was looking north from just south of Eagle Street.
7/11/41 19252

Lochner's Home Bakery on James Street had a very tempting display.
7/10/47 22768

Dillard's Restaurant at 501 Jay Street had entertainment by Leon "Bub" Coakley at the piano.
5/8/47 22903

Neighborhood "mom and pop" stores were essential parts of the city.

Warren at Sunset 7/8/47 23069

1501 Seymour Avenue 6/12/44 21141

1501 Steuben Street 6/16/47 23021

The Bleecker Street area had many small businesses and many furniture stores. It was almost another downtown.

847 Bleecker Street 3/11/43 20377A

647 Bleecker Street 12/7/43 20785

The DeRosa building at 662-668 Bleecker Street housed a Ben Franklin 5 and 10 cent store, several offices (including that of Attorney George Schiro, chronicler of the early history of Utica's Italian community) and a large social hall on the third floor.
9/2/40 18253

McQuade and Bannigan was one of the many coal dealers in Utica. The Delaware, Lackawanna & Western Railroad delivered coal to their trestle on the south side of Noyes Street. Both the office with its covered truck scales and the trestle came down for the North-South Arterial.
10/18/40 18492

11/13/40 18618A

The tracks of the New York, Ontario & Western followed the former route of the Chenango Canal to serve coal dealers and other industries. All except the one next to the building at right were replaced by the North-South Arterial. This view looks south from the corner of Sunset Avenue and Wager Street.
6/2/41 19239

Hess Lane was next to the New York Central's busy four-track main line. The Durr packing plant was across the tracks.
5/21/41 19176 (damaged)

Rail sidings serving industries on Broad Street were frequently in use. This view looked west near the Foster bedspring factory.
3/29/42 19900

Dump trucks and concrete mixers lined up in front of the American Hardwall Plaster Company on Broad Street, ready for the postwar building boom.
5/24/49 26191

A new gas station owned by Thomas Welch opened at the corner of North Genesee Street and Herkimer Road.
5/13/42 20024

5/13/42 20028

The Utica Braves played night baseball at McConnell Field, next to the Barge Canal in North Utica. Also known as "splinter haven," this modest stadium was replaced by the Thruway entrance.
4/26/40 17814

North Genesee Street had a long history as a commercial strip. A huge gasholder at Harbor Point dominated the horizon to the west.
8/20/40 18190

Wells Gardens was an early real estate development in the Town of Deerfield. This was the west side of Walker Road between today's Beaumond Place and Northwood Drive. Remodelling and the growth of large trees have altered this scene almost beyond recognition today.
11/12/41 19653

The Suburbs and Farther Out

The suburbs were places apart, even when their borders were contiguous with Utica's. They were served—but less frequently—by the same streetcar and bus lines as the city. Beyond the suburbs was "real" country, with farms and woods, cows and chickens. Each suburb was perceived as different and unique with its own character, ambience and history.

Stevenson's Drug Store and Deming's news-stand were in the middle of New Hartford village.
4/26/49 26101 (damaged)

On a wet February day in New Hartford, one lonely man was waiting for the trolley on Genesee Street near Merritt Place.
2/13/41 18964

A year later, the trolley tracks had been removed from the right-of-way parallel to Genesee Street in New Hartford.
4/3/42 19925

The Utica Country Day School in New Hartford was a popular private school. After the war, it housed Mohawk Valley Technical Institute, and later, Notre Dame High School, before being taken down for apartments.
8/21/42 20156

Ibbotson house, 85 College Street 8/40 18177

These homes were all in the Village of Clinton.

2 Woodlawn Place 8/40 18178

Billingham house, 5 Utica Street 8/40 18172

These houses on Sauquoit Street in New York Mills were but two of many originally built for mill workers and owned by the textile companies. Note the imposing Greek Revival mansion in the background, once the home of one of the mill owners.
12/2/40 18695

6/18/40 17933

The single trolley track on Main Street in New York Mills went past modest homes and the "upper" school.

6/18/40 17925

This car was parked on Walker Road, about one mile north of the city limits. The view was to the south, toward Utica.
7/30/41 19295

This truck was travelling on the old River Road near Marcy State Hospital.
5/14/47 22925

The 1949 graduating class of Maynard School in Marcy posed proudly.
6/23/49 26324 (damaged)

The veranda of Hart's Hill Inn was a quiet place to sit and look over the valley.
7/1/49 26414 (damaged)

The Eisele farm near Deansboro included a frame house with a central chimney, typical of the architecture transplanted from New England to Central New York in the late 1700s and early 1800s. This was one of the few farms pictured in the Rhoades collection.
6/4/41 19200

Mapledale Corners on the way north to Barneveld showed plenty of wide open country covered in snow.
2/10/44 20895A-B

The Brunner Manufacturing Company used an assembly line to speed the making of compressors.
5/41 19069

The Work We Did

Work was always an important part of our lives and Russell Rhoades was called to photograph many of the industrial and commercial areas. Although Utica was still known for its textile mills, that industry had already started its long decline, with World War II providing a brief reprieve. But we also had foundries and radiators and tools and souvenirs and machine guns and emblems and pumps and compressors and much more in the area if not strictly within the city limits.

Cooking gas was manufactured from coke and steam and stored in huge tanks near the harbor. Most homes were heated with coal which several companies supplied from trestles near one of the railroads. More affluent citizens heated with oil which was delivered by barge during the warm months and stored in tank farms near the canal for winter use.

The former home of Governor Horatio Seymour was a part of the Divine Brothers' Whitesboro Street plant, against a backdrop of the gas works.
6/30/42 20096

This shiny new Divine grinder was installed at the Utica Steam Engine & Boiler Works on Whitesboro Street.
5/22/44 21097

Wrenches were turned out in great numbers at this plant of Utica Drop Forge Company.
3/30/44 20965D

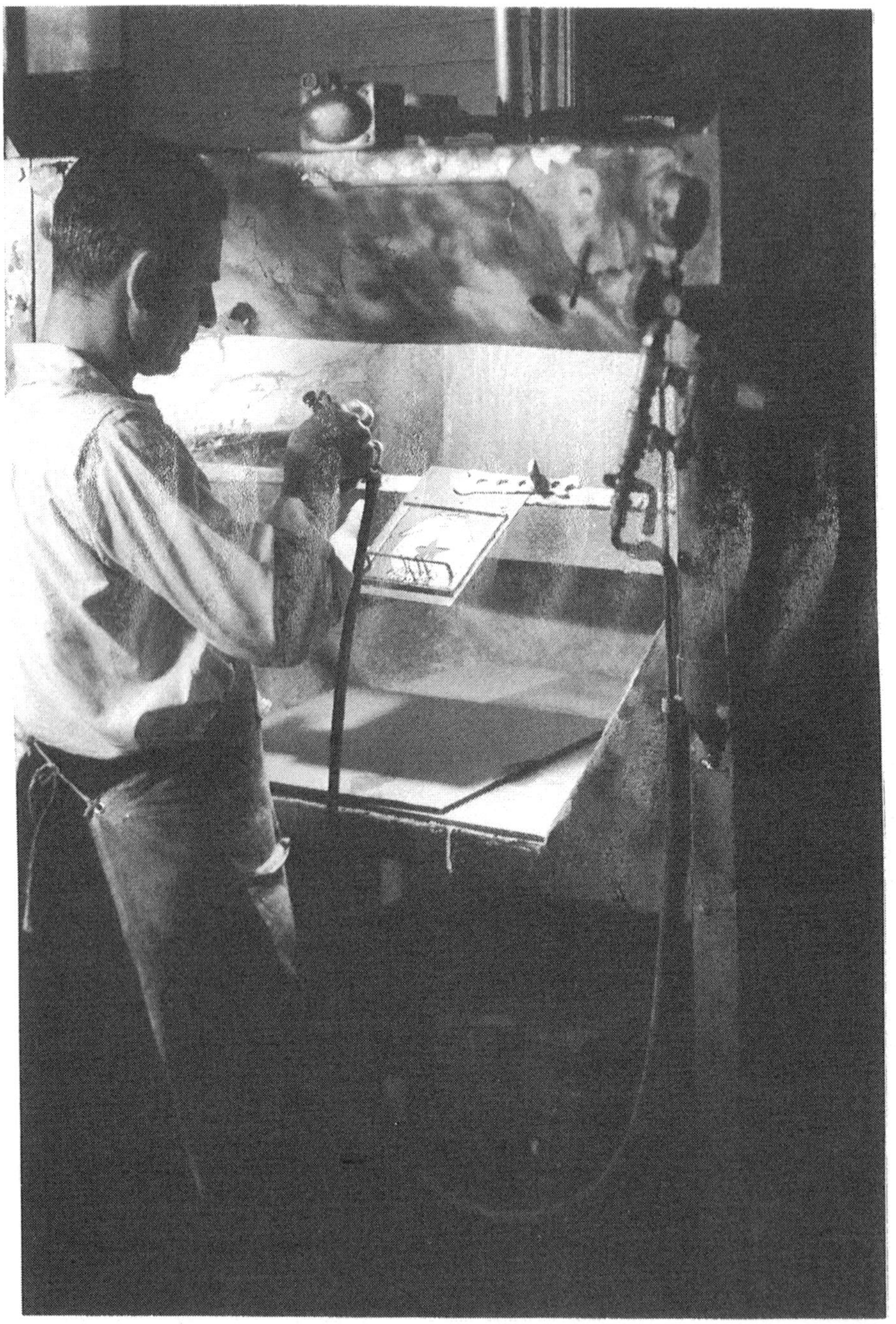

Enamelling, grinding and polishing operations were photographed at the American Emblem Company in New Hartford, which made metal emblems for automobiles, appliances, machinery, etc.
4/25/47 22719K

4/25/47 22719U

4/25/47 22719P

If you bought a souvenir in Denver or New Hampshire, it might have been made at the Madmar Quality Company in West Utica.
3/4/47 22745

The tool room at Richardson-Boynton was secured behind a screen.
4/9/41 19086

These generators were at furnace manufacturer Richardson-Boynton's plant in Whitesboro.
4/9/41 19091

D. B. Smith's "Indian" pumps—made to fight brush and forest fires—were field tested, here at Remsen.

5/19/47 23004A-C

Carding machines—used to prepare cotton for spinning—stood in long rows in the Utica and Mohawk Cotton Mills.
3/11/49 25892

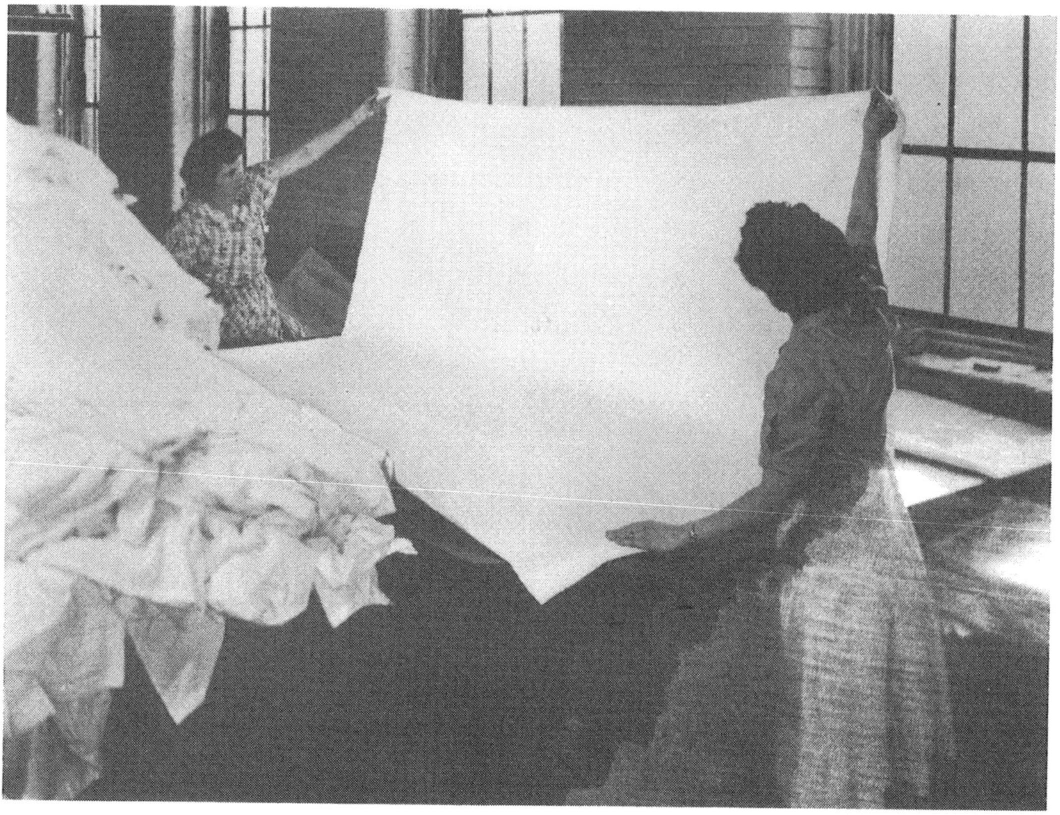

Inspectors check the finished sheets at the same mills.
3/11/49 25892 (damaged)

11/1/43 20098R

11/1/43 20098N

11/1/43 20098A

The foundry at Utica Radiator was one of the few places in Utica where blacks and whites worked together in the 1940s.

Further operations at Utica Radiator. 11/1/43 20098B

11/1/43 20098O

11/1/43 20098D

Durr Packing Company was north of the New York Central tracks, east of the Barnes Avenue overpass.
9/21/47 19499

Rhoades photographed packages for many clients, including the West End Brewery.
7/8/49 26396 (damaged)

The Regal Boys' Suit Company factory was at 524 Catherine Street.
3/13/42 19844

The brightly lit salesroom of the Gordon Davis agency at 1711 Genesee Street was very tempting to postwar motorists.
3/1/47 22746B

The Way We Went

For long distance travel and freight hauling, we had the New York Central Railroad (including the northern branches to Watertown, Lake Placid, Malone and Montreal). The New York, Ontario & Western (O&W) and the Delaware, Lackawanna & Western (DL&W) Railroads both reached Utica from the south, but by World War II, the O&W was already "freight service only." Our last streetcars rolled into history in May 1941.

Trucks were used for local deliveries and were a source of real pride for their owners. The automobile was no longer a curiosity; increasing use brought an increasing number of traffic accidents which the Rhoades photographers were often called upon to document.

The bus fleet of the New York State Railways—former operators of the local trolley system—was ready to carry passengers to work or play. The garage was on Main Street opposite Union Station and the Hieber Building, later the Children's Museum. These pictures may have been occasioned by accidents or the delivery of new buses, such as the shiny Twin Coach on the opposite page, one of 37 purchased in 1941 to replace the last local electric streetcars.

3/26/43 20416

3/20/44 20951A

6/18/41 19274A

The State Barge Canal was frequently busy. Oil and other bulk products traveled by this slower but cheaper method.
6/20/44 21148A

Union Station was a busy place. The west-bound Empire State Express—running with no fewer than sixteen cars—pulled into Utica on a chilly day. On the opposite platform, passengers waited for an eastbound train. Freight tracks were to the north.
6/20/44 21148B

Heating fuel was delivered by truck, and there were many companies to supply the city's needs. Some area residents used oil or kerosene, but in the 1940s many still burned coal.
5/22/44 21093

9/20/41 19576

1927 Reo 11/14/40 18809

1935 Plymouth 2/22/44 20902

1941 Pontiac 3/3/41 19009

1939 Dodge 11/20/40 18808

Major collisions and minor fender-benders, whatever the cause or the season, Rhoades photographed them all.

1936 Dodge "woodie" station wagon
8/26/42 20158B

1946 Chevrolet 3/1/47 22747

1939 Pontiac (Note World War II gas ration stickers on the windshield.)
4/4/44 20988

1936 Plymouth 1/29/41 18855

P.F. Scheidelman and Sons distributed beer by truck from their headquarters at 519-525 Varick Street.
5/10/40 17874

Utica Club beer and ale were delivered in style by a new Mack tractor pulling a streamlined Fruehauf trailer, both with red body, white lettering and yellow wheels.
8/25/47 23152

This year-old 1939 Buick was recorded for insurance purposes—and posterity—at the entrance of Truax's Oneida Square Service. The quality of this professional photograph, made on an 8 x 10-inch negative, is a far cry from the Polaroids snapped by insurance adjusters on similar occasions today.
7/16/40 18033

Here's another way to go, after it's fixed!
6/24/41 19215

This girl was selling defense stamps at Woolworth's just a few weeks before Pearl Harbor.
10/4/41 19560A

The War We Helped to Win

A second world war had started in Europe in 1939. Even before the United States was officially at war, support for the Allied cause could be expressed by the purchase of savings bonds and stamps; there was a big effort to involve everyone. Social events to support the rapidly increasing number of men in our armed forces were popular, as well as those for the British War Relief.

After the Pearl Harbor attack in 1941, Uticans supported our country's involvement wholeheartedly. Many women went to work in the war industries to replace men. (Utica had always had a large female work force in the textile mills.) Many parties were held for men and women in the armed forces. Other activities were designed to keep up morale on the home front.

Companies that exceeded government assigned quotas were awarded an "E" for Excellence flag. Many Utica industries were proud to display these banners.

This was a memorable day at Horrocks-Ibbotson on Whitesboro Street. The building was originally built by the Saturday Globe.
12/30/41 19754

Savings Bonds could be purchased at any bank or post office. This was the Savings Bank of Utica.
1/22/43 20318

These ladies met at the Hotel Utica to plan a ball for the benefit of the United Service Organizations and British War Relief.
10/17/41 19604A

4/7/44 20980

These ladies came to work at Divine Brothers to help the war effort.

4/7/44 20981

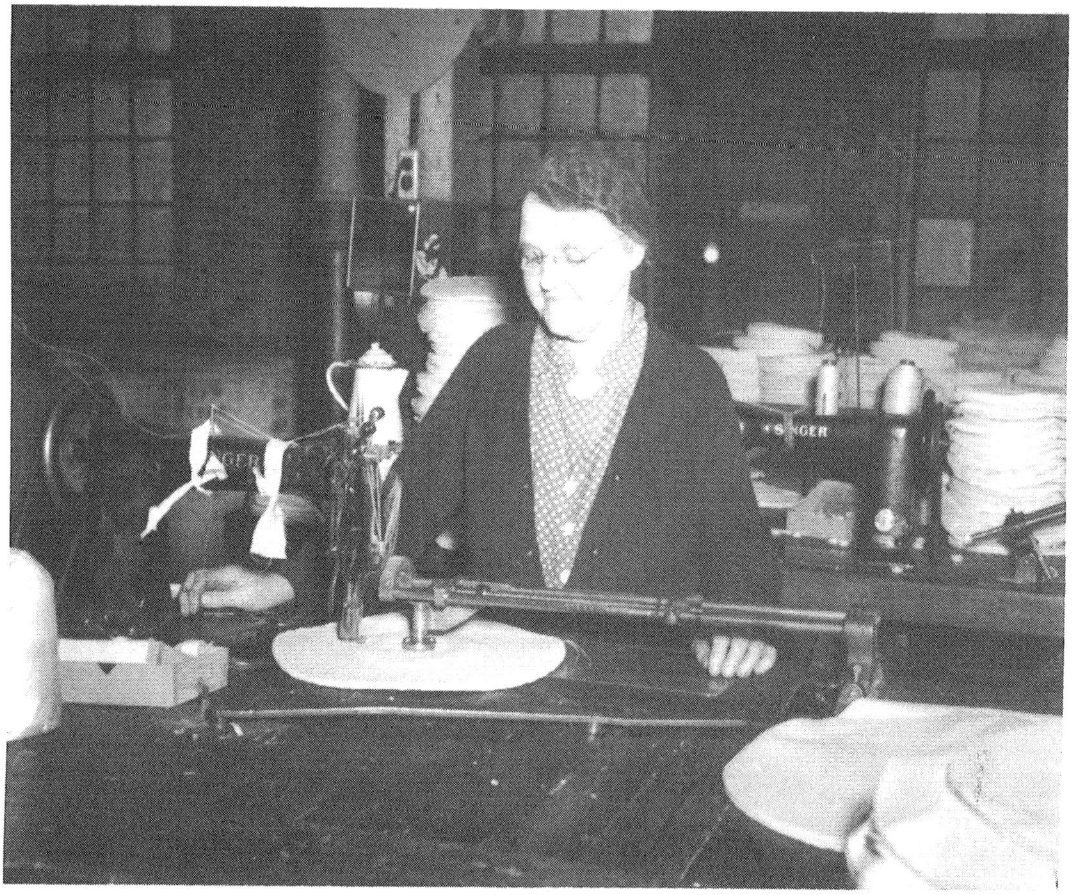

4/7/44 20982

4/7/44 20983

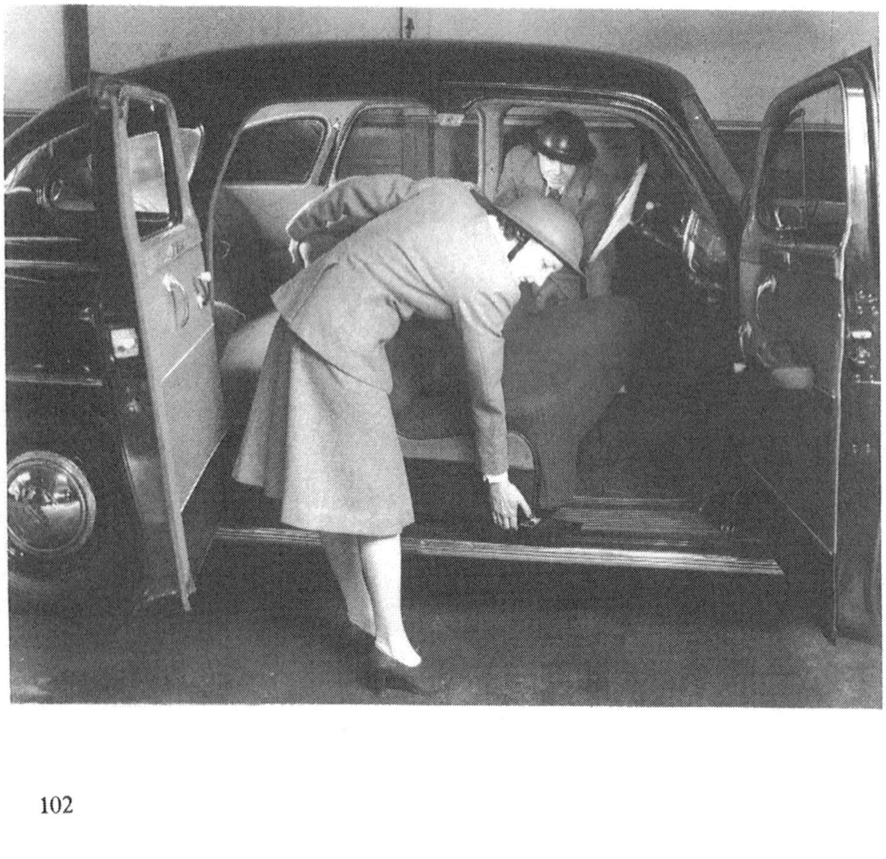

Store windows took on a patriotic theme for the holidays. Rudolph's Jewelry at 176 Genesee Street offered many gifts suitable for members of the armed forces.
12/1/43 20315

Well-dressed volunteers, preparing for air raids on Utica, demonstrated the conversion of a Plymouth sedan to an ambulance.
4/24/42 19942

Brunner's received one of the first "E for Excellence" flags in this area.
12/8/42 20250

Woolworth's promoted "National Letter Writing Week" with a display of stationery and fountain pens.
10/6/42 20196

Nice, New Cars Can't Be Sold for Another Year

Some of the brand new (1942) automobiles in a shipment of 155 received by Harry Heiman Inc. are parked in a Lafayette St. lot, covered with snow and ice, waiting for indoor storage room. Government orders prevent their sale until January, 1943, at the earliest (unless rules are changed), but the tires (four to each car) may be sold through rationing boards.

DEALER GETS 155 NEW CARS

Brand new automobiles, 155 of 'em, valued at approximately $200,000, have been received in Utica during the last few days. But they cannot be sold before January, 1943, at the earliest.

It's just like getting a big package around New Year's Day, with the label, "Don't open before Christmas."

Only these aren't Christmas presents. They had to be paid for at the time shipments were made, and now that the 155 cars of various models have arrived, the problem is to find storage space.

70 Remain Outdoors

All but 70 of the cars have been moved to warehouses and store rooms of Harry Heiman, Inc., but those 70 are still outdoors in a parking lot, covered with snow and ice at present.

"U. S. of America, Priorities Division, Public Notice. The United States, in the interest of national defense, has subjected this car to priority and rationing regulations. It may not be sold and delivered pursuant to said regulations and may not be defaced. Violators of the regulations are subject to all penalties prescribed herein."

Then appears a space showing the motor number, serial number and date.

Shorn of Chromium

The new cars are war-time vehicles, all being shorn of chromium and other fancy trimmings. Each car has four tires, but no spare.

While sale of the new cars is forbidden until January, 1943, tires and tubes on the cars may be sold to "an appropriate agency as directed" and the dealer or distributor would be compensated to the extent of the wholesale price of the tires and tubes, Heiman said.

Must Await Permission

A telegram received by Heiman from the Chrysler Corporation says it is acting under orders of the price administrator, Leon Henderson, in directing that the dealer or distributor "refrain from selling the passenger cars so shipped until specific permission to sell is granted."

Such permission will be granted, the message said, "when it is deemed in the public interest to do so, but probably not earlier than January, 1943."

One storehouse in Hotel St. and another in Lafayette St., are now utilized by Heiman, in addition to the company's own sales and service headquarters at 324 Lafayette. Efforts are being made to find another location to store the 70 cars now in a parking lot.

Plymouth dealer Harry Heiman had this newspaper article copied, explaining why the few automobiles on hand early in the war could not be sold to eager would-be buyers.
7/28/42 20121

Guards at Savage Arms raised the flag daily and thoroughly checked all trucks entering and leaving the plant.
7/2/43 20539

This was a real milestone—the 1,000,000th Thompson gun made at Savage Arms.
7/2/43 20570

Women took over many jobs at Savage.
7/2/43 20539

7/2/43 20539

Quitting time at Savage was always welcome.
7/2/43 20539

Afterword

What else is in the Rhoades collection?

The scope of this book is limited to 1940-1949, but the complete collection of surviving Russell Rhoades negatives extends to 1960, depicting even more aspects of the economic and social life of the Utica area. The Society hopes to publish at least one more volume of Rhoades photos, to cover the 1950-1960 period.

Rhoades took pictures for a wide range of local clients. Their photographs illustrated catalogs, brochures and newsletters, served as evidence for court cases and insurance claims, and only by happenstance captured a great deal of history in the process. Subject matter included, but was not limited to, individual buildings, street and highway scenes, local industries, motor vehicles, and groups of people and individuals.

What did the OCHS have to do to catalog the collection?

The Oneida County Historical Society took physical possession of the Rhoades collection in August 1982 for examination. We received the negatives, together with enough old steel transfer files to hold about half of the negatives, plus a card index.

Immediately upon receiving the collection, we took steps to organize it. Our part-time cataloger, Francis Cunningham, put the negatives back into numerical order and made a list of the numbers received. Unfortunately, some negatives had suffered water damage and been discarded after Rhoades' basement was flooded during fires on either side of their Devereux Street shop. Negatives dating back into the 1930s may have been made on nitrate film and discarded due to deterioration or their notorious flammability. As a result, some items listed in the index no longer exist, but at least we know what we received in the beginning.

Until 1985, we made only limited use of the collection, pending resolution of legal technicalities regarding the donation. Joseph Skane, president of the company, finalized the gift in November 1985.

Meantime, in the spring of 1985, Peg Hassett—an OCHS member and secretary of our board of trustees at the time—volunteered to further organize the collection. Mrs. Hassett is a retired science teacher from the Whitesboro Central School District. She has been active in historical organizations (including serving as president of the OCHS 1990-1992). A long-time member of the Utica Camera Club, she is a serious amateur photographer with a permanent home darkroom. All in all, she brought a very appropriate combination of talents and interests to this project.

Mrs. Hassett's work included:

1. examining individual negatives for retention or disposal, based on historical significance and/or physical condition, in consultation with Society Director Doug Preston,
2. refiling the retained negatives in new, acid-free paper envelopes and transcribing all information from the old kraft-paper envelopes,
3. making prints from unidentified negatives (a very small percentage of the total) for exhibition and identification by the public,
4. making prints of pictures of immediate interest or use to the Society,
5. further indexing, particularly of pictures of buildings, by street address, or by other categories.

Russell T. Rhoades & Company did significant amounts of photography for a few firms outside Oneida County. We felt it unlikely that persons researching those firms would ever find their way to the OCHS given the present state of photographic finding aids. And because of limited space and resources, such negatives were offered to the appropriate county historical societies or to the surviving customers.

Mrs. Hassett worked an average of one full day per week for over three years, including time spent with the collection in the Society's quarters plus work at home on the index and in the darkroom, *prior to* starting work on this book. The late Mary Louise Quayle contributed many hours to assisting in the transfer of negatives and transcription of information from old to new envelopes.

Society volunteer George White assisted with filing and, as a lifelong Utica resident, with identification of some of the negatives. Barton Rasmus of the Mohawk Motorcades antique auto club identified and dated the old cars. Attorney David Peet and Frank Aceto of the Oneida County Clerk's Office map room helped us to identify and locate Wells Gardens on Walker Road, surprisingly the most vexatious research problem we encountered. Volunteer Marjorie Freytag has further refined the index to the many photos of buildings on Genesee and other principal streets. Frank Devecis, formerly associated with the advertising firm of Moser & Cotins (a Rhoades client), provided valuable guidance with the initial layout of this book.

What is the value of the Rhoades collection and who uses it?

Russell T. Rhoades & Company made photographs for commercial, documentary or legal purposes, not for artistic reasons. However, they worked with skill, using mostly large-format (5″ x 7″ or 8″ x 10″) films and professional cameras. Therefore, the resulting images are well composed, perfectly focused, very clear and highly detailed. If these pictures are not art, then they are fine specimens of photographic craftsmanship.

The Rhoades photos illustrate a period that is only beginning to be represented in the collections of the Oneida County Historical Society. Furthermore, they record subjects that are probably unrecorded elsewhere.

The Society regularly uses pictures in historical publications and exhibitions, as well as for reference. Pictures can be copied onto slides, for use both in lectures in the Society's quarters and in programs throughout the community. In many cases, pictures can serve the Society as a practical substitute for the acquisition of large objects of only specialized interest, such as machines or other industrial products.

For those original customers that are still in business, old pictures can be valuable benchmarks of progress in technology or corporate growth and change. Individuals frequently contact the Society looking for pictures of old buildings. In the case of many demolished buildings, these pictures may be the only visual record of their existence while for buildings still standing, they may provide valuable information for restoration.

Some thoughts on the value of historical photographs in general

There has been an explosion of interest in historical photographs in the past 25 or 30 years. Books published by American Heritage, Time-Life and others, television documentaries such as Ken Burns' monumental series on the Civil War, and museum exhibitions from the Smithsonian Institution to the smallest local historical societies have all featured photographs as dramatic "windows on the past."

The Library of Congress received many early photographs for copyright purposes, as well as images created under such federal programs as the Farm Security Administration, many of which have become nationally-recognized icons of American history. The New York State Historical Association, just over the hill in Cooperstown, became a pioneer in the preservation of local photographs when it acquired more than 50,000 glass plates from the village's Smith and Telfer studios in the early 1950s. The George Eastman House in Rochester is home to vast collections, not only of early cameras, but of historically significant photographs, and it has pioneered in the application of computer and laser disc technology to the cataloging of photographs.

Along with this growing interest in, and appreciation of, photographs has come a dramatic rise in prices paid for photographs in the art and antique markets in recent years. The works of such nationally-known early photographers as Matthew Brady and A.J. Russell, or more recent camera artists such as Ansel Adams, regularly fetch large sums in toney galleries and auction houses. Even a photograph taken for reference purposes by a painter—Charles Sheeler's shot of the driving wheels of a New York Central "Hudson" steam passenger locomotive—sold for a record sum a few years ago.

This escalation of prices sometimes presents a dilemma for local museums and historical societies seeking to acquire local photographs to document the history of their own communities. Large collections of historical photographs, primarily of local significance, belong in local historical collections where they can be made accessible to local people.

But some individuals and dealers assume that, because one photograph of a particular subject, or from a particular era, sells for a large price in the competitive atmosphere of a big-city auction room, therefore all similar photos should do likewise. They may assume that because a nationally-known institution such as the Library of Congress or the George Eastman House has a few photographs in its collections from a particular locality, or because a talented local photographer had some pictures published in national magazines, that such an institution would be willing to pay large sums to acquire any and all other photos from that locality or by that local photographer.

Nationally-prominent institutions, or even individual collectors blessed with deep pockets, may be attracted to selected images from large local collections, but few have the means, the space, or the desire to acquire very many *complete* collections numbering hundreds or thousands of items. Smaller, local institutions rarely have any more than token funds available for acquisitions, and must depend on donations from people who put posterity ahead of profit.

As a result, such collections in the hands of dealers are sometimes sold piecemeal, scattered and their historical integrity lost forever. Or they languish in obscurity, deteriorating, of use to no one, and doing no honor to the skill or memory of the talented individuals who created them. This was the case with the Rhoades collection until it came to the Society's attention. It is probably still the case with some others. Fortunately however, Rhoades' owner Joe Skane shared our enthusiasm for his negatives and was happy to turn them over to us. The fate of some other collections remains to be determined.

What may be forgotten is that, in acquiring a major photo collection such as that of Russell T. Rhoades & Company, a historical agency also takes on a major responsibility, financial and otherwise. When a major collection is brought into a historical repository, the work—and the expense—are just beginning. As indicated above, considerable resources—human, financial, and physical—are all needed in order to organize, catalog, preserve, house and publish a collection such as this.

The 100-plus images in this book were selected from more than 10,000 negatives in the Rhoades collection, all of which received equal basic treatment in terms of acid-free envelopes, catalog cards and initial time spent in sorting and cataloging. More significant items are receiving additional treatment. This would have been impossible without many hours of donated labor and the help of all of the individuals and agencies who contribute to the Society's support for general operations and special projects such as this.

Copies

Copies of the photographs in this book, and in other collections of the Oneida County Historical Society, are available by special order. Please write to the Society at 1608 Genesee Street, Utica, NY 13502-5425 or call (315) 735-3642 for a current photo reproduction policy and price list.